BERNIE

THE BLOB SEAL

Nate Addlestone

ISBN 979-8-88644-206-9 (Paperback)
ISBN 979-8-88644-207-6 (Digital)

Covenant Books
11661 Hwy 707
Murrells Inlet, SC 29576
www.covenantbooks.com

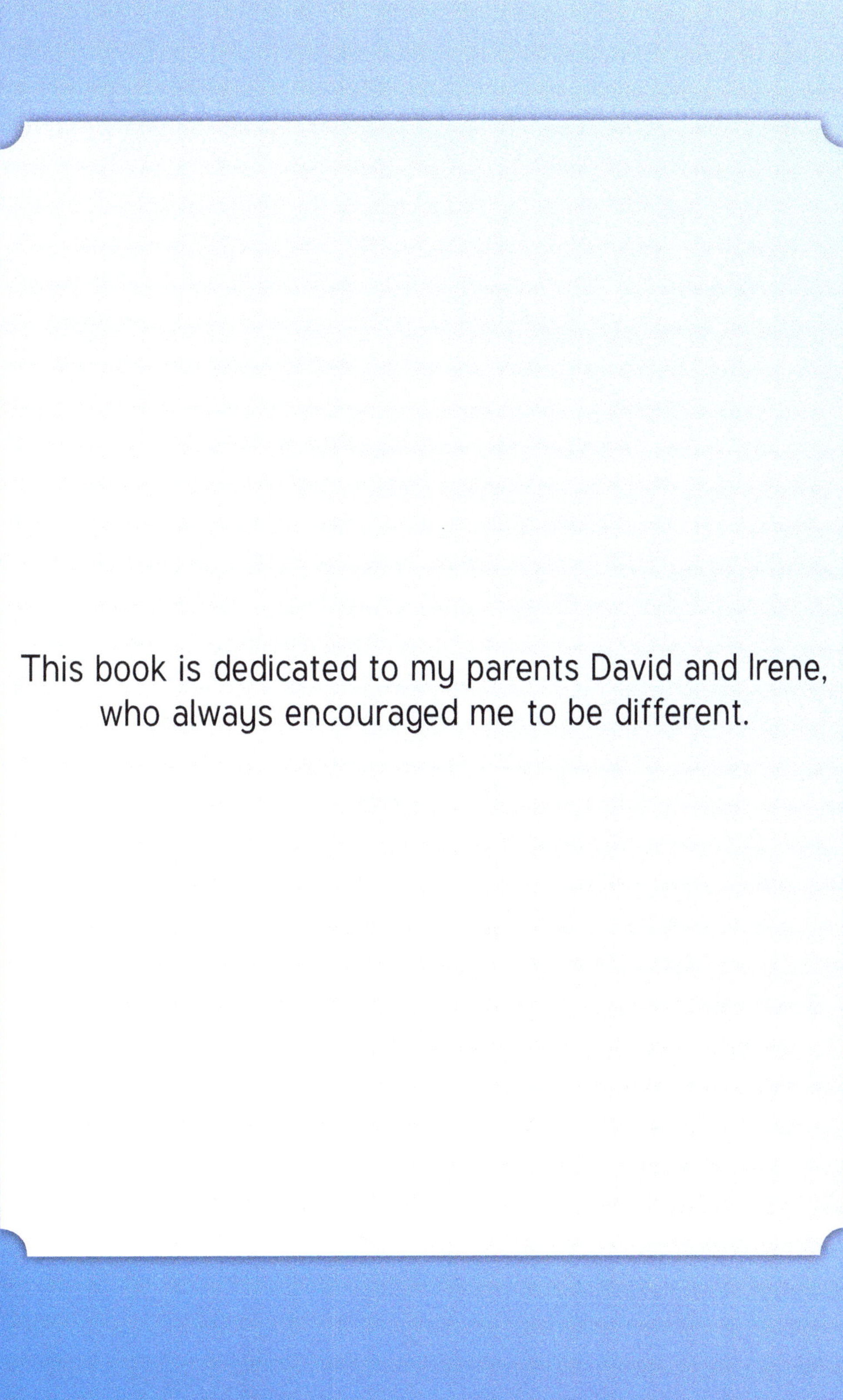

This book is dedicated to my parents David and Irene, who always encouraged me to be different.

This is a story about a large seal named Bernie,
The tale of his love and growth is quite the journey.

Bernie was a blob seal, different from the rest,
As soon as he was born, the chubbiest
part of his body was his chest!

Because he was different, the other
seals would call him "fat,"
Instead of swimming and playing, he
would just stay remaining sat.

When in the water, seals can hold their
breath for up to two hours,
Poor Bernie, when he tried to fit through the ice,
he got stuck and just looked overpowered.

"Why am I so different from the other
seals?" he would ask his mom and dad,
"Seals, just like people, come in all shapes,
sizes, and colors. No reason to be mad!"

All seals have a thick layer of blubber
to keep them warm in icy water,
The bigger you are, the longer you remain hotter!

Bernie finally fit through ice, so now he
could play and swim through the water,
Where did seals come from? Surprisingly,
they evolved from bears and otters!

But the other seals didn't want to play
with him because he was so thick,
But a seal swam up to Bernie and
introduced his name as Rick.

"I'm an elephant seal," Rick told Bernie. "We
are equal in size, so don't have any fears."
No matter the size or shape of a seal,
they can live for up to thirty years.

The number of different species
for seals can be over thirty.
"Whether in the arctic or tropics, the water
they swim in will always be murky."

So Bernie had a new best friend that
made him so joyous and happy,
They swam past the other rude and mean
seals who had called him fatty.

But Bernie noticed something
different about his friend, Rick,
Something that made him glide through the
water easier and make it look so slick.

Rick told him that seals could navigate
through dark waters with ease,
The whiskers on their face helped
them swim through the seas.

Then Bernie asked, "I thought the only
animals with whiskers were cats?"
"No, no," Rick explained. "Seals also
have them, and that is a fact!"

Their whiskers also help seals
detect and follow their prey,
Seals prefer to feast on fish, squid, or birds, catching
any of those will certainly make their day.

So Rick taught Bernie how to better travel and swim,
Because of pollution, seals have to
be ready to move on a whim.

Among the things affecting seals is
pollution from chemicals and trash,
Not to mention global warming also is enough abuse
to make anyone run away quickly in a flash!

"That's why some seals have to migrate hundreds
of miles each year in search of food," Rick said.
Especially for seals who are elephant
and blob, they need to travel extra far
to make sure they can stay fed.

"Wow, I didn't know a seal's life would
be so hard," Bernie exclaimed.
With so many different species across the world,
you would think the seals would be famed!

So Bernie and Rick became the best of
friends, spending all their time together.
They would play tag, swim around, and even chase
other seals, no matter the time or weather.

"See," Bernie's parents told him. "You
will always find someone like you, no
matter your shape, color, or size."
Whether a toothpick, elephant, or in between,
you should never feel ashamed about
yourself enough to wear a disguise.

ABOUT THE AUTHOR

Nate Addlestone currently lives in Washington, D.C., after graduating from Elon University with a bachelor's degree in communications and obtaining his master's degree in journalism from the University of Miami. He has always had a passion for creative writing, is an accomplished poet, and takes pride in his storytelling among all age groups. All these factors helped him with his continuous pursuit of journalism and knowledge toward equality.